To help make feeling different feel ok

To my little Luca,
you are my inspiration for this book
and I am so proud of you.
x

Luca the lion couldn't eat meat,
not for lunch, nor for dinner
or even a treat.

Since cubhood he'd struggled
to have just a lick,
as each time he tried it he
ended up sick!

'IT'S NOT FAIR!'

Luca moaned as he watched
his friends munch,
on the big juicy meat joints
they had for their lunch.

At bedtime that night, he spoke of his day.
With sadness he asked

'Why am I this way?'

**'Luca...
there's plenty of foods
you can eat'**

Said Tersha, his Mum,
as she dried off his cheek.

**'It's not your friend's faults
that their tummies like meat,
your tum is just different
and so you're *UNIQUE!*'**

'What you have is an allergy
you are not alone,

there are many, like you,
who are allergy prone.'

At school Luca frowned
as his lunchtime grew near.

Milo, the monkey, sat close in his chair.

'Luca,
what's wrong?'

asked Luca's best mate

'I'm feeling sad,
feeling different,
not great...

I wish, oh I wish,
I could eat what you do
why am I different?
I'm not like you!'

'Luca?' said Milo
'Let me tell you this,
I am a monkey
what food's on our list?

BANANAS!

That's right!
that's what we should eat,
but my MUM cannot stand them
she'd rather eat meat!'

'They make her all spotty and blotchy and red,

and she has to, immediately, go straight to her bed!'

'So you see Luca, buddy, it isn't just you
my Mum has an allergy, just like you do.

Please don't be sad, or worried, or glum
you are friendly and funny...now let's

GO HAVE SOME FUN!'

So, off the boys went
and Luca felt good.

Milo had helped him
think less about food.

Instead Luca thought of
what he could do...

like

DANCING... ...

and

SUPER

... CLIMBING...

HERO MOVES!

At home he told Mum
what had happened at school.

How Milo's Mum, Vicky,
had allergies too.

'See my darling, it's true,
you are **NOT ALONE**,

there are those, like you,
who are allergy prone.'

Next day, back at school,
Luca felt not so bad,
'til Cali, the cat,
showed him what she had.

A bottle of milk
was her drink for that day.

Luca felt jealous, once again not ok.

See, it wasn't just meat
that made Luca feel queasy,
but milk also made
Luca's tummy uneasy.

Since cubhood he'd struggled
to have but a sip,
as whenever he did
he'd always been SICK!

'Cali?' said Luca

'It just isn't fair!'

As he sat, frustrated,
on the edge of his chair.

'I wish, how I wish,
I could drink what you do.

Why am I different?
I'm not like you!'

Cali moved in closer and gave him a smile,
put her hand upon his and they sat for a while.

'Luca?' said Cali

'Can I tell you this, I am a cat,
what drink's on our list?

MILK!

Yes of course!
that's what us cats drink,
but my Dad he can't stand it
it makes his

FEET STINK!'

'They get hot and then sweaty and soon pong like old cheese,

and it isn't too long 'til his nose starts to **SNEEZE!'**

'So you see Luca, pickle,
it isn't just you,
my Dad has an allergy
just as you do.

Please don't be jealous
it's a waste of your day,
you're kind and so caring
now let's...

GO AND PLAY!'

So off they both skipped
and Luca felt GOOD!
Cali had helped him
to change his bad mood.

Now Luca was smiling
and feeling so HAPPY,
running around
being silly with Cali.

Back home he told Dad
what had happened at school,
how Cali's Dad, Gary, had allergies too.

**'See, your Mum told the truth
you are not alone,
there are others, like you,
who are allergy prone.'**

The next time he saw
his friend's, Milo and Cali,
he said

'THANK YOU SO MUCH!'
for making him happy.

For being great mates
and helping him see...

what's important, what matters,

now he felt... CARE FREE!

Luca the Lion couldn't eat meat,
not for lunch, nor for dinner
or even a treat!

Since cubhood he'd struggled
to have just a lick
but...
did it bother him?

'NO... NOT ONE BIT!'

Printed in Great Britain
by Amazon

47443220R00020